Puffin
Rescue!

Rob Waring, *Series Editor*

HEINLE
CENGAGE Learning

Australia • Brazil • Japan • Korea • Mexico • Singapore • Spain • United Kingdom • United States

Words to Know

This story is set in Iceland. Iceland is a country in Europe. The story happens in a small town called Heimaey [heɪmaɪ]. The town is on the south coast of Iceland.

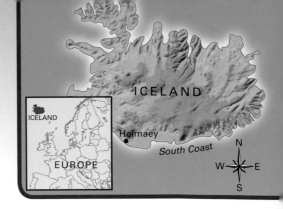

A **Puffins.** Read the paragraph. Then complete the sentences with the underlined words.

This story is about puffins. Puffins are a kind of bird. The largest groups of puffins live in Iceland. Very young puffins are called pufflings. As they grow older, the pufflings try to fly away. However, sometimes, the pufflings become confused. They get lost and can't find the sea. Groups of people help these pufflings. These groups are called 'puffling patrols.' They rescue the pufflings and help them find the water.

1. _____ are a kind of bird that lives in Iceland.
2. _____ are young puffins.
3. _____ are groups of people that help puffins.
4. _____ means to save or keep safe.
5. A person or animal that does not understand something is _____.

A Puffling — **A Puffin**

B **A Seaside Town.** The town of Heimaey is by the sea. Here are some things you can find in a seaside town. Label the picture with the correct words.

beach	cliff	dock	pier	sea

3. _____

4. _____

2. _____

1. _____

5. _____

Einar and his sister Andrea are going to the beach to do a very important job. They have a box with them. Inside their box they have two helpless **orphans**[1] that they found on the streets of Heimaey, Iceland. What are they? They're young puffins!

Einar and Andrea hope to help the birds. They want to give them a **second chance**[2] at life. Einar explains why they want to do it. "They don't **survive**[3] if they stay in the town," he says. "Cats and dogs eat them, or they just die. It's really good to save them," he adds.

---

[1]**orphan:** a person or animal that has no mother or father
[2]**second chance:** another try
[3]**survive:** stay alive

🎧 CD 1, Track 05

The children of Heimaey have been saving young puffins, or pufflings, for a long time. At the end of every summer, they help the lost pufflings find their way to the sea. It has become a tradition in the area around Heimaey.

Even the parents support the children and what they do. One parent reports, "They have to save the birds. If they don't do it, they die." She then adds that the children enjoy their work. "They find it very **exciting**,"[4] she says.

---

[4]**exciting:** fun and interesting

Predict

Answer the questions. Then scan page 8 to check your answers.

1. Why do the pufflings get lost?

2. What do the children do with lost pufflings?

While it is very exciting for the children, it may not always be enjoyable for the pufflings. However, it does save the young birds from danger. The children take the lost pufflings to the beach. Then they throw the pufflings into the air and watch them fly away. But why do the pufflings get lost in the first place?

When the young puffins are old enough, they leave their homes in the cliffs. They try to fly out to sea. But sometimes the lights from the town of Heimaey confuse them. This causes problems for pufflings. When this happens, the young puffins don't fly out to sea; they fly into the town!

Once they're in the town, the confused birds **crash into**[5] things. The people there find them on the streets of the city. That's when the children of Heimaey come to help. That's when they start having puffling patrols!

---

[5]**crash into:** run into; hit

Sequence the Events

What is the correct order of the events? Write numbers.

_____ The pufflings get lost.

_____ The pufflings leave the cliffs.

_____ The children find the pufflings.

_____ The children release the pufflings.

Each night at the end of the summer, moms and dads lead groups of children through town. They look for these lost pufflings. They use **flashlights**[6] to search the ground near buildings and street lights.

The pier is usually a good place to look for pufflings. When the children see a bird, they run to pick it up. They rescue the pufflings so they don't have to stay on the streets for the night. It's hard work, but it's fun, too.

---

[6]**flashlight:** a small light people can carry

puffling patrol

flashlight

A puffling patrol is looking for a lost puffling. Where is it?

At midnight, Olaf Holm and his six-year-old son Andrew are looking for pufflings. They look carefully around the docks. A half an hour later, they have a bird!

Olaf tells his story, "We came across the **parking lot**[7] and saw the **silhouette**.[8] [It] looked like a little puffin and sure enough—there he was! Right in the middle of the parking lot. We jumped out and we got him!"

---

[7]**parking lot:** a place where people keep their cars
[8]**silhouette:** shape or outline (of a puffin)

The next day, the puffling patrols take the rescued birds to the seashore. The children point the birds towards the ocean and release them. The children have a great time, but they must learn how to release the pufflings safely.

First, they must hold the puffin correctly. Next, they have to use the right style to throw the bird. It's almost like throwing a ball. Finally, they release the young puffin towards the sea! After that, it's up to the little puffin to swim or fly to safety.

Whether they swim or fly away, no one knows how this man-made problem really affects the puffins. There are eight to ten million puffins in Iceland. That's more than anywhere else in the world!

Fortunately, the yearly **search-and-rescue**[9] in Heimaey has become a big tradition. There, even lost pufflings get a second chance—all because of the strong arms and big hearts of the children of Heimaey!

---

[9]**search-and-rescue:** a plan to look for and save (puffins)

After You Read

1. What are Einar and his sister going to do at the beach?
   A. help some people
   B. clean the beach
   C. help some small birds
   D. play with puffins

2. According to page 4, why don't pufflings survive in Heimaey?
   A. People hurt them.
   B. Cars kill them.
   C. It's too cold.
   D. Animals eat them.

3. In paragraph 1 on page 7, 'they' refers to:
   A. pufflings
   B. orphans
   C. children
   D. cats

4. If the lost pufflings don't get help, _____ will die.
   A. it
   B. those
   C. they
   D. them

5. Where is the pufflings' home?
   A. the streets
   B. the cliffs
   C. the beach
   D. the docks

6. What's a good heading for page 8?
   A. Saving Lost Pufflings
   B. Birds Fly Home
   C. Town Lights
   D. Out to Sea

7. The puffling patrol does each of these EXCEPT:
   A. search near buildings
   B. check the beach
   C. go out at night
   D. take flashlights

8. On page 12, the word 'hard' in the phrase 'hard work' means:
   A. difficult
   B. boring
   C. dangerous
   D. terrible

9. In what direction should the puffins fly to safety?
   A. toward the town
   B. near the beach
   C. out to sea
   D. toward the lights

10. Why is rescuing puffins so popular in Iceland?
    A. Iceland's national bird is the puffin.
    B. People in Iceland love birds.
    C. Search-and-rescue is a hobby there.
    D. Iceland has a lot of puffins.

11. A person with a 'big heart' is each of these EXCEPT:
    A. kind
    B. confused
    C. friendly
    D. nice

12. The purpose of the last paragraph is to show that:
    A. Children have strong arms in Heimaey.
    B. Many puffins won't get a second chance.
    C. Children can make a difference in the world.
    D. The lost pufflings are safe in Iceland.

TELT Times

WHALE CAUGHT IN THAMES

As Martin Hewes looked out a train window in the middle of London, he thought he saw a whale in the River Thames. "That can't be!" he said to himself. While this kind of occurrence is not common, Hewes was wrong. Somehow, a northern bottlenose whale was caught in the River Thames. Whales don't usually appear in the middle of London. It's over twenty miles from the sea. The whale was about 20 feet long and weighed nearly 10,000 pounds. The appearance of the whale was exciting for the thousands of people who came to see it and to observe the rescue attempts.

A northern bottlenose whale was found in the River Thames.

Rescuers place the whale on a ship to try to save it.

No one is quite sure how the whale got into the difficult situation. Whales usually travel in groups and don't normally come near land. Scientists assume that this one lost contact with its group and became confused. The whale got into trouble when it entered the River Thames. The water wasn't deep enough for it to move easily. A whale is used to being in 2000 feet of water, and this water was less than 15 feet deep. The rocks at the base of the river cut into the whale. The rescue team said that as the whale tried to move around, it crashed into the sides of the river.

The next day, the rescue team attempted to lead the whale out toward the sea, but it was unable to move by itself. Its only chance for survival was to be put on a ship and carried out to sea. As the hours passed, the situation became even more serious. Unfortunately, in the end, the whale died. Many animal rescues are successful, but experiences like this one show us that no matter how hard we try, humans can't always change the course of nature.

CD 1, Track 06

Word Count: 319
Time: _____

Vocabulary List

beach (3, 4, 8)

cliff (3, 8, 11)

confuse (2, 8, 10)

crash into (10)

dock (3, 14)

exciting (7, 8)

flashlight (13)

orphan (4)

parking lot (14)

pier (3, 12)

puffin (2, 4, 7, 8, 14, 16, 18)

puffling patrol (2, 10, 12, 13, 16)

puffling (2, 7, 8, 10, 11, 12, 13, 14, 16, 18)

rescue (2, 12, 16, 18)

sea (3, 8, 16)

search-and-rescue (18)

second chance (4)

silhouette (14)

survive (4)